BIRD ON A WIRE 4

CHELSEA HOTEL #2 9

DRESS REHEARSAL RAG 14

EVERYBODY KNOWS 24

FAMOUS BLUE RAINCOAT 32

FIRST WE TAKE MANHATTAN 38

HEY THAT'S NO WAY TO SAY GOODBYE 21

I'M YOUR MAN 51

JOAN OF ARC 46

SEEMS SO LONG AGO, NANCY 62

SO LONG, MARIANNE 58

SUZANNE 76

TAKE THIS WALTZ 65

TOWER OF SONG 84

WHO BY FIRE 81

BIRD ON A WIRE

WORDS AND MUSIC BY LEONARD COHEN

THE LEONARD COHEN COLLECTION

AMSCO PUBLICATIONS
NEW YORK/LONDON/SYDNEY

CR
10.95 X

Cover photograph by Dominique Issermann
Arrangements by Frank Metis

This book Copyright © 1991 by Amsco Publications,
A Division of Music Sales Corporation, New York, NY.

Order No. AM 85549
US International Standard Book Number: 0.8256.1314.0
UK International Standard Book Number: 0.7119.2731.6

EXCLUSIVE DISTRIBUTORS:
Music Sales Corporation
225 Park Avenue South, New York, NY 10003 USA
Music Sales Limited
8/9 Frith Street, London W1V 5TZ England
Music Sales Pty. Limited
120 Rothschild Street, Rosebery, Sydney, NSW 2018, Australia

Printed in the United States of America by
Vicks Lithograph and Printing Corporation

If I, if I have been un-kind,

I hope that you can just let it go by.

If I, if I have been un-true,

I hope you know it was nev-er to you. More like a

She cried to me, "Hey, why not ask for more?" More like a bird on the wire,_____ like a drunk in a mid-night choir, I have tried in my way to be free._____

ritard.

CHELSEA HOTEL #2

WORDS AND MUSIC BY LEONARD COHEN

keep track of each fall - en rob - in. I re -

mem - ber you well in the Chel - sea Ho - tel, That's

all, I don't think of you that of - ten.

ritard.

Additional Lyrics

2. I remember you well in the Chelsea Hotel,
   You were famous, your heart was a legend.
   You told me again you preferred handsome men,
   But for me you would make an exception.
   And clenching your fist for the ones like us
   Who are oppressed by the figures of beauty,
   You fixed yourself, you said, "Well, never mind,
   We are ugly but we have the music."
   Chorus

3. I don't mean to suggest that I loved you the best,
   I can't keep track of each fallen robin.
   I remember you well in the Chelsea Hotel,
   That's all, I don't think of you that often.

DRESS REHEARSAL RAG

WORDS AND MUSIC BY LEONARD COHEN

2. **A** There's no hot water and the cold is running thin,
    Well, what do you expect from the kind of places you've
    been living in?

    B Don't drink from that cup, it's all caked up and cracked
    along the rim,
    That's not electric light, my friend, that is your
    vision growing dim.

    C Cover up your face with soap, there, now you're Santa Claus,
    And you got a gift for anyone who will give you his applause.

    D I thought you were a racing man, ah, but you couldn't take
    the pace.
    That's a funeral in the mirror, and it's stopping at your face.

    E That's right, it's come to this.
    Yes, it's come to this,
    And wasn't it a long way down?
    Ah, wasn't it a strange way down?

3. **A** Once there was a path and girl with chestnut hair,
    And you passed the summers picking all of the berries that
    grew there.

    B There were times she was a woman, there were times she was
    just a child,
    And you held her in the shadows where the raspberries grow wild.

    C And you climbed the twilight mountains, and you sang about the
    view,
    And ev'rywhere you wandered, love seemed to go along with you.

    D That's a hard one to remember, yes, it makes you clench your fist,
    And the veins stand out like highways all along your wrist.

    E And yes, it's come to this.
    It's come to this,
    And wasn't it a long way down?
    And wasn't it a strange way down?

4. **A** You can still find a job, go out and talk to a friend,
    On the back of every magazine, there are those coupons you
    can sand.

    B Why don't you join the Rosicrucians? They will give you
    back your hope,
    You can find your love with diagrams on a plain brown
    envelope.

    C But you've used up all coupons, except the one that seems
    To be written on your wrist along with several thousand
    dreams.

    D Now Santa Claus comes forward, that's a razor in his mitt,
    And he puts on his dark glasses, and he
    ⊕ shows you where to hit.

    E And then the cameras pan, the stand-in stunt man,
    dress rehearsal rag.
    It's just the dress rehearsal rag,
    You know this dress reharsal rag,
    It's just the dress rehearsal rag.

Hey That's No Way To Say Goodbye

Words and Music by Leonard Cohen

bye.

2. I'm not
3.   I

Additional Lyrics

2. I'm not looking for another
   As I wander in my time.
   Walk me to the corner,
   Our steps will always rhyme.
   You know my love goes with you
   As your love stays with me,
   It's just the way it changes
   Like the shoreline and the sea.
   But let's not talk of love or chains
   And things we can't untie,
   Your eyes are soft with sorrow,
   Hey, that's no way to say goodbye.

3. I loved you in the morning,
   Our kisses deep and warm,
   Your hair upon the pillow,
   Like a sleepy golden storm.
   Yes, many loved before us,
   I know that we are not new,
   In city and in forest,
   They smiled like me and you.
   But let's not talk of love or chains
   And things we can't untie,
   Your eyes are soft with sorrow,
   Hey, that's no way to say goodbye.

Everybody Knows

Words and Music by Leonard Cohen and Sharon Robinson

Moderately, with a steady beat

Verses

optional eighth note pattern continues throughout

1. Ev-ery-bod-y knows that the dice are load-ed. Ev-ery-bod-y rolls with their fin-gers crossed. Ev-ery-bod-y

knows.   Ev-ery-bod-y knows.   That's   how it

goes.   Oh,   ev-ery-bod-y   knows. _____

Additional Lyrics

4. And everybody knows that it's now or never.
   Everybody knows that it's me or you.
   And everybody knows that you live forever
   When you've done a line or two.
   Everybody knows the deal is rotten:
   Old Black Joe's still pickin' cotton
   For your ribbons and bows. And everybody knows.

5. Everybody knows that the plague is coming.
   Everybody knows thats it's moving fast.
   Everybody knows that the naked man and woman
   Are just a shining artifact of the past.
   Everybody knows the scene is dead,
   But there's gonna be a meter on your bed
   That will disclose what everybody knows.

6. And everybody knows that you're in trouble.
   Everybody knows what you've been through,
   From the bloody cross on top of Calvary
   To the beach of Malibu.
   Everybody knows it's coming apart:
   Take one last look at this Sacred Heart
   Before it blows. And everybody knows.

FAMOUS BLUE RAINCOAT

WORDS AND MUSIC BY LEONARD COHEN

four in the morn — ing, the end of De — cem — ber,

I'm writ-ing you now just to see if you're bet-ter.

New York is cold, but I like where I'm liv-ing, The

mus - ic on Clin -ton Street all through the eve - ning.

I hear that you're build -ing your lit - tle

night that you planned to go clear.

Sin - cere - ly, L. Co - hen.

ritard. *p*

Additional Lyrics

2. The last time we saw you, you looked so much older,
   Your famous blue raincoat was torn at the shoulder.
   You'd been to the station to meet ev'ry train,
   You came home without Lili Marlene.
   And you treated my woman to a flake of your life,
   And when she came back, she was nobody's wife.
Chorus: Well, I see you there with a rose in your teeth, one more thin gypsy thief.
   Well, I see Jane's away, she sends her regards.

3. And what can I tell you my brother, my killer,
   What can I possibly say?
   I guess that I miss you, I guess I forgive you,
   I'm glad you stood in my way.
   If you ever come by here for Jane or for me,
   Well, your enemy is sleeping and his woman is free.
Chorus: Yes, thanks for the trouble you took from her eyes.
   I thought it was there for good, so I never tried.

Coda: And Jane came by with a lock of your hair,
   She said that you gave it to her,
   That night that you planned to go clear.
   Sincerely, L. Cohen.

First We Take Manhattan

Words and Music by Leonard Cohen

Additional Lyrics

From D.S.
I don't like your fashion business, mister.
I don't like these drugs that keep you thin.
I don't like what happened to my sister.
First we take Manhattan, then we take Berlin.

(Bridge):
I'd really like to live beside you, baby.
I love your body and your spirit and your clothes.
But you see that line there moving through the station?
And I told you, and I told you,
I told you I was one of those,

And I thank you for those items that you sent me:
The monkey and the plywood violin.
I practiced every night and now I'm ready.
First we take Manhattan, then we take Berlin. *(To Coda)*

JOAN OF ARC
WORDS AND MUSIC BY LEONARD COHEN

1. Now the flames, they fol - lowed Joan of Arc

As she came rid - ing through the dark.

No moon to keep her ar - mor bright, No

A wed-ding dress or some - thing white to

wear up - on ___ my swol - len ___ ap - pe -

tite." ___

Chorus:

La la la, la la la, la la la la la

Additional Lyrics

2. Well, I'm glad to hear you talk this way,
   You know I've watched you riding ev'ry day.
   Something in me yearns to win
   Such a cold and lonesome heroine.
   "And who are you," she sternly spoke
   To the one beneath the smoke.
   "Why I'm fire," he replied,
   "And I love your solitude, I love your pride."
   Chorus

3. "Then fire make your body cold,
   I'm gonna give you mine to hold."
   Saying this, she climbed inside
   To be his one, to be his only bride.
   And deep into his fiery heart,
   He took the dust of Joan of Arc.
   And high above the wedding guests,
   He hung the ashes of her wedding dress.
   Chorus

4. It was deep into his fiery heart
   He took the dust of Joan of Arc.
   And then she clearly understood,
   If he was fire, oh, then she must be wood.
   I saw her wince, I saw her cry,
   I saw the glory in her eye.
   Myself, I long for love and light,
   But must it come so cruel and, oh, so bright!
   Chorus

I'm Your Man

Words and Music by Leonard Cohen

G

claw at your heart,__ and I'd tear at your sheet. I'd say, please,__

E

A

_ please,__ I'm your man.__

Bm

No chord

And if you've got to sleep for a mo - ment

Em

on the road,_ I will steer for you.__ And if you want to

D

No chord

So Long, Marianne
WORDS AND MUSIC BY LEONARD COHEN

Moderately slow, in 2

It's time that we be-gan___ to laugh and cry and cry and laugh a-bout it all a-gain.

2. Well,

Additional Lyrics

2. Well, you know that I love to live with you,
   But you make me forget so very much.
   I forget to pray for the angel,
   And then the angels forget to pray for us.
   Chorus

3. We met when we were almost young,
   Deep in the green lilac park.
   You held on to me like I was a crucifix,
   As we went kneeling through the dark.
   Chorus

4. Your letters, they all say that you're beside me now.
   Then why do I feel alone?
   I'm standing on a ledge, and your fine spider web
   Is fastening my ankle to a stone.
   Chorus

5. For now I need your hidden love,
   I'm cold as a new razor blade.
   You left when I told you I was curious,
   I never said that I was brave.
   Chorus

6. Oh, you're really such a pretty one.
   I see you've gone and changed your name again,
   And just when I climbed this whole mountainside
   To wash my eyelids in the rain.
   Chorus

7. O your eyes, well, I forget your eyes,
   Your body's at home in every sea.
   How come you gave away your news to everyone,
   That you said was a secret for me?
   Chorus

Seems So Long Ago, Nancy

Words and Music by Leonard Cohen

Additional Lyrics

2. It seems so long ago,
    none of us were strong.
Nancy wore green stockings,
    and she slept with everyone.
She never said she'd wait for us,
    although she was alone.
I think she fell in love for us
    in nineteen sixty-one,
    in nineteen sixty-one.

3. It seems so long ago,
    Nancy was alone.
A forty-five beside her head,
    an open telephone.
We told her she was beautiful,
    we told her she was free.
But none of us would meet her in
    the House of Mystery,
    the House of Mystery.

4. And now you look around you,
    see her everywhere.
Many use her body,
    many comb her hair.
And in the hollow of the night,
    when you are cold and numb,
You hear her talking freely then,
    she's happy that you've come,
    she's happy that you've come.

Take This Waltz

WORDS BY LEONARD COHEN/GARCIA LORCA
MUSIC BY LEONARD COHEN

Suzanne

WORDS AND MUSIC BY LEONARD COHEN

Additional Lyrics

2. And Jesus was a sailor
   When he walked upon the water,
   And he spent a long time watching
   From his lonely wooden tower.
   And when he knew for certain
   Only drowning men could see him,
   He said,"All men will be sailors then
   Until the sea shall free them."
   But he himself was broken,
   Long before the sky would open.
   Forsaken, almost human,
   He sank beneath your wisdom like a stone.
   And you want to travel with him,
   And you want to travel blind,
   And you think maybe you'll trust him,
   For he's touched your perfect body
         with his mind.

3. Now Suzanne takes your hand,
   And she leads you to the river.
   She is wearing rags and feathers
   From Salvation Army counters.
   And the sun pours down like honey
   On our lady of the harbour.
   And she shows you where to look
   Among the garbage and the flowers.
   There are heroes in the seaweed,
   There are children in the morning,
   They are leaning out for love,
   And they will lean that way forever.
   While Suzanne holds the mirror.
   And you want to travel with her,
   And you want to travel blind,
   And you know that you can trust her,
   For she's touched your perfect body
         with her mind.

Who By Fire

Words and Music by Leonard Cohen

Additional Lyrics

2. And who in her lonely slip,
   Who by barbiturate?
   Who in these realms of love,
   Who by something blunt?
   Who by avalanche,
   Who by powder?
   Who for his greed,
   Who for his hunger?
   And who shall I say is calling?

3. And who by brave ascent,
   Who by accident?
   Who in solitude,
   Who in this mirror?
   Who by his lady's command,
   Who by his own hand?
   Who in mortal chains,
   Who in power?
   And who shall I say is calling?

Tower Of Song

Words and Music by Leonard Cohen

Moderately, with a steady beat

1. Well, my friends are gone and my hair is grey. I ache in the plac-es where I used to play. And I'm cra-zy for love,

I'll be speak-ing to you sweet-ly from a win-dow in the Tow-er of Song. —

Additional Lyrics

2. I said to Hank Williams, "How lonely does it get?"
Hank Williams hasn't answered yet.
But I hear him coughing all night long,
A hundred floors above me in the Tower of Song.

3. I was born like this, I had no choice.
I was born with the gift of a golden voice.
And twenty-seven angels from the Great Beyond,
They tied me to this table right here in the Tower of Song.

4. So you can stick your little pins in that voodoo doll.
I'm very sorry, baby, doesn't look like me at all.
I'm standing by the window where the light is strong.
They don't let a woman kill you, not in the Tower of Song.

5. Now you can say that I've grown bitter, but of this you may be sure:
The rich have got their channels in the bedrooms of the poor.
And there's a mighty judgment coming, but I may be wrong.
You see, you hear these funny voices in the Tower of Song.